HERBAL REMEDIES FOR PTSD

Unlocking Healing Paths And Nature's Resilience For Lasting Well-Being, Holistic Healing And Healthy Lifestyle

DR. CARDEN KYRIE

DISCLAIMER

The only goal of this book is informational. Every effort has been taken by the author and publisher to ensure that the information provided is accurate. But the material in this book is given "as is," without any express or implied representation, warranty, or condition as to its accuracy, completeness, or suitability for any particular purpose.

Any loss, damage, or injury resulting from using the information in this book, or from any action or decision made as a result of such use, will not be covered by the author's or publisher's liability. It is recommended that readers seek the assistance of a certified specialist for guidance specific to their situation.

The opinions and viewpoints conveyed in this book belong to the author and may not necessarily represent the official stance or policies of any specified organizations or people. Any likeness to real-life occurrences, places, or people—living or deceased—is wholly coincidental.

No specific product, service, or therapy discussed in this book is endorsed by the author or publisher. Any reference to goods or services is made only for informative reasons and is not intended as a recommendation or endorsement.

Before making any judgments or acting on any information, readers are urged to independently confirm it all. Any unfavorable effects or repercussions arising from the usage of the material included in this book are disclaimed by the author and publisher.

By using this book, you consent to absolving the publisher and author of any and all claims, obligations, or losses resulting from your use of the material in it.

I appreciate your cooperation and understanding.

TABLE OF CONTENTS

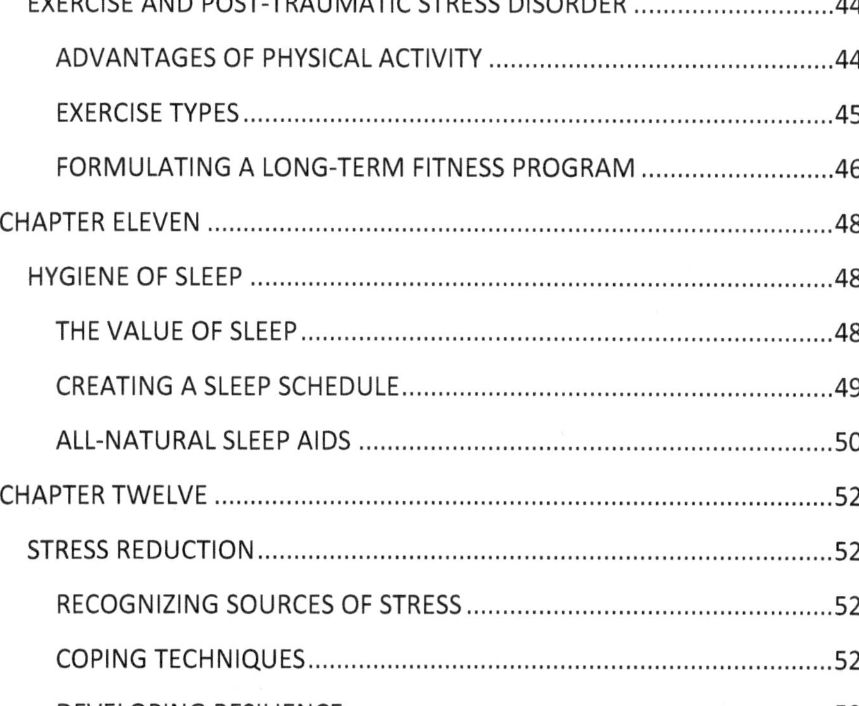

CHAPTER ONE

INTRODUCTION TO PTSD

WHAT PTSD IS DEFINED AS

A mental health disorder known as post-traumatic stress disorder (PTSD) can arise in people who have gone through or observed a terrible event. A traumatic incident, such as a natural disaster, a major accident, a terrorist attack, war or conflict, rape, or other violent personal assault, can cause post-traumatic stress disorder (PTSD), according to the American Psychiatric Association.

Many symptoms, including intrusive memories, flashbacks, nightmares, and extreme anxiety, can seriously interfere with a person's day-to-day functioning and are indicative of post-traumatic stress disorder (PTSD).

FREQUENCY AND SIGNIFICANCE

PTSD is very common and has a significant impact on people from a wide range of backgrounds and demographic groupings. Numerous studies have shown that the prevalence of PTSD varies based on variables like the kind of trauma one has experienced, one's level of resilience, and the availability of support networks. It can impact people of various ages, genders, and cultural origins and is not restricted to any particular population. Beyond the person, PTSD influences relationships, employment, and general quality of life. PTSD sufferers may find it difficult to keep a job, build and maintain connections with others, and participate in hobbies they used to like.

THE VALUE OF COMPREHENSIVE METHODS

Effective therapy and support for post-traumatic stress disorder (PTSD) require an understanding of the significance of holistic methods. A person's physical, mental, and emotional well-being are all intertwined, and holistic methods recognize that trauma impacts a person's life in many ways. A variety of therapies that go beyond conventional therapy techniques are included in holistic approaches to treating PTSD. These could consist of yoga, art therapy, mindfulness exercises, and other complementary and alternative therapies. Holistic approaches acknowledge that trauma healing encompasses not just mental but also physical and spiritual aspects of recovery, and they strive to improve total resilience and well-being by treating the full person.

Holistic approaches also emphasize the value of a multidisciplinary, team-based approach to treatment. To provide a thorough and personalized care plan, collaboration between mental health specialists, medical professionals, social workers, and other support services is required. To address the complex and multifaceted character of PTSD, a more comprehensive and individualized approach is achieved through the merging of holistic methodologies with evidence-based treatments.

Knowing what constitutes post-traumatic stress disorder (PTSD), identifying its impact and frequency, and appreciating the value of holistic therapies are essential to treating this mental health issue. A more all-encompassing and integrative approach to supporting persons impacted by PTSD can be promoted by individuals and professionals working together to promote healing and resilience through the adoption of a holistic worldview.

CHAPTER TWO

AN OVERVIEW OF SYMPTOMS OF PTSD

REGAINING SYMPTOM EXPERIENCE

who have Post-Traumatic Stress Disorder (PTSD) frequently exhibit a variety of symptoms that fall into four major groups. Re-experiencing symptoms, such as intrusive and disturbing memories, flashbacks, or nightmares connected to the traumatic incident, fall within the first cluster. Reminders or cues connected to the trauma might set off these symptoms, causing an elevated emotional response and a sensation of reliving the terrible event. Reliving symptoms can seriously interfere with day-to-day functioning since they make it difficult for sufferers to distinguish between their prior trauma and their current situation.

SYMPTOMS OF AVOIDANCE

Avoidance behaviors are another well-known cluster of symptoms associated with PTSD. People will do everything in their power to stay away from things, people, or activities that remind them of the traumatic experience. This avoidance can even extend to talking about the unpleasant event or expressing feelings associated with it. Relentless attempts to avoid upsetting stimuli might result in social disengagement and a feeling of separation from other people. Although avoidance symptoms are initially used as coping strategies, they can also make a person feel more alone and make it more difficult for them to process and incorporate the trauma into their story of life.

SYMPTOMS OF HYPERAROUSAL

Hyperarousal symptoms are the third cluster of PTSD presentations, characterized by heightened physiological arousal. This heightened state of alertness can result in difficulties concentrating, irritability, insomnia, and an exaggerated startle response. Individuals with hyperarousal symptoms may be easily startled by loud noises or sudden movements, reflecting an ongoing state of hypervigilance.

These symptoms contribute to a sense of constant danger and an inability to relax, impeding the individual's overall well-being and quality of life.

COGNITIVE AND MOOD SYMPTOMS

Cognitive and mood symptoms form the final cluster of PTSD manifestations. Individuals may experience negative changes in their thought patterns and beliefs, leading to persistent feelings of guilt, shame, or a distorted sense of blame related to the traumatic event. Cognitive symptoms can also include memory impairments, difficulty concentrating, and a sense of a foreshortened future, where individuals may struggle to envision a fulfilling life ahead. Mood symptoms often involve persistent feelings of sadness, hopelessness, or emotional numbness, further contributing to the overall impact of PTSD on mental health.

It's important to note that PTSD symptoms can vary in intensity and duration, and not everyone who experiences trauma will develop the disorder.

Additionally, the interplay of these symptom clusters can create a complex and challenging experience for individuals affected by PTSD. Seeking professional help, such as therapy and counseling, is crucial for effective management and recovery from PTSD.

CHAPTER THREE
CAUSES AND TRIGGERS
TRAUMATIC EVENTS

Traumatic events can have profound and lasting effects on an individual's mental and emotional well-being. These events, which are often distressing and overwhelming, can range from personal experiences such as accidents, violence, or loss of a loved one, to broader societal traumas like wars or natural disasters. The impact of traumatic events can vary widely from person to person, influenced by factors such as resilience, coping mechanisms, and pre-existing mental health conditions.

Trauma can act as a catalyst for mental health issues, triggering conditions like post-traumatic stress disorder (PTSD) or exacerbating existing vulnerabilities.

BIOLOGICAL FACTORS

Biological factors play a crucial role in shaping an individual's susceptibility to various mental health conditions. Genetics, for instance, can contribute to the predisposition for certain disorders. A family history of mental health issues may increase the likelihood of an individual developing similar conditions. Additionally, neurochemical imbalances in the brain, such as irregularities in neurotransmitter levels, can contribute to the onset of mental health disorders. The interplay between genetics and neurobiology underscores the complex nature of mental health, where a combination of genetic predisposition and biological processes can influence an individual's vulnerability.

ENVIRONMENTAL INFLUENCES

Environmental influences encompass a wide array of external factors that can impact an individual's mental health. Socioeconomic status, access to education, and exposure to environmental toxins are just a few examples. Living in a supportive and nurturing environment can promote positive mental health, while adverse conditions, such as poverty or discrimination, may contribute to the development of mental health issues. The quality of one's living conditions, including housing stability and community support, plays a crucial role in shaping mental well-being. Additionally, exposure to chronic stressors, such as ongoing financial difficulties or social isolation, can contribute to the triggering or exacerbation of mental health conditions.

PSYCHOSOCIAL CONTRIBUTORS

Psychosocial contributors refer to the social and psychological factors that influence an individual's mental health. These can include interpersonal relationships, family dynamics, and cultural influences. Social support networks play a vital role in buffering the impact of stressors and traumas. Positive social connections and a strong support system can enhance resilience and contribute to better mental health outcomes.

On the other hand, dysfunctional family dynamics, strained relationships, or a lack of social support may increase vulnerability to mental health issues. Cultural factors, including societal norms and expectations, can also shape an individual's perception of mental health and influence their willingness to seek help or disclose their struggles.

The causes and triggers of mental health issues are multifaceted, involving a complex interplay of traumatic events, biological factors, environmental influences, and psychosocial contributors. Understanding these various elements is crucial for developing effective prevention strategies, interventions, and support systems to promote mental well-being.

CHAPTER FOUR

CONVENTIONAL TREATMENTS

PSYCHOTHERAPY

Psychotherapy is a therapeutic approach that involves talking to a trained mental health professional to explore and understand the thoughts, feelings, and behaviors that may be contributing to psychological distress. This form of treatment aims to provide individuals with a safe and supportive environment to express themselves, gain insight into their problems, and develop coping strategies.

Psychotherapy can take various forms, such as psychodynamic therapy, humanistic therapy, and behavioral therapy, tailoring the approach to the specific needs of the individual. The collaborative nature of psychotherapy allows for the development of a therapeutic relationship that fosters personal growth and improved mental well-being.

MEDICATIONS

Medications play a crucial role in the conventional treatment of various mental health conditions. Psychotropic medications, such as antidepressants, anxiolytics, and antipsychotics, are commonly prescribed to alleviate symptoms associated with mood disorders, anxiety disorders, and psychotic disorders. These medications work by targeting neurotransmitters in the brain, modulating their levels to restore a balance that may be disrupted in certain mental health conditions. While medications can be effective in managing symptoms, they are often used in conjunction with other therapeutic approaches, such as psychotherapy, to address the underlying causes of mental health disorders and promote holistic recovery.

COGNITIVE-BEHAVIORAL THERAPY (CBT)

Cognitive-behavioral therapy (CBT) is a widely practiced form of psychotherapy that focuses on identifying and challenging negative thought patterns and behaviors. The core principle of CBT is that our thoughts, feelings, and behaviors are interconnected, and by changing distorted thought patterns, individuals can modify their emotional responses and behaviors. CBT is goal-oriented and time-limited, often involving structured sessions where individuals learn to recognize and reframe maladaptive thoughts. This therapeutic approach has been proven effective in treating various mental health conditions, including depression, anxiety disorders, and post-traumatic stress disorder (PTSD).

EYE MOVEMENT DESENSITIZATION AND REPROCESSING (EMDR)

Eye Movement Desensitization and Reprocessing (EMDR) is a specialized form of psychotherapy designed to alleviate the distress associated with traumatic memories. Initially developed for the treatment of PTSD, EMDR has been applied to other mental health conditions as well. The therapy involves a structured eight-phase approach that includes the identification of target memories, desensitization through bilateral stimulation (typically guided eye movements), and the development of adaptive coping mechanisms. EMDR is believed to facilitate the processing of traumatic memories, reducing their emotional intensity and allowing individuals to integrate these experiences more adaptively. While the exact mechanisms of EMDR are not fully understood, numerous studies support its efficacy in trauma treatment.

Conventional treatments for mental health conditions encompass a range of approaches, including psychotherapy and medication. Cognitive-behavioral therapy and Eye Movement Desensitization and Reprocessing are specific psychotherapeutic techniques that have demonstrated effectiveness in addressing various mental health issues. The combination of these modalities, tailored to the individual's needs, offers a comprehensive approach to treating mental health disorders and promoting overall well-being.

CHAPTER FIVE

LIMITATIONS OF CONVENTIONAL TREATMENTS

SIDE EFFECTS

Conventional treatments, while often effective in managing various medical conditions, are not without their limitations. One significant drawback lies in the realm of side effects. Many traditional medications and therapies come with a range of adverse reactions that can negatively impact patients' well-being. These side effects may vary in severity, from mild discomfort to more serious complications that can compromise the overall quality of life for individuals undergoing treatment.

For example, chemotherapy, a common conventional treatment for cancer, is notorious for its side effects such as nausea, fatigue, and hair loss. Similarly, pharmaceutical drugs used to manage chronic conditions like hypertension or diabetes may lead to dizziness, gastrointestinal issues, or even more severe complications. The challenge, therefore, is to strike a balance between the benefits of these treatments and the potential harm caused by the associated side effects.

ACCESSIBILITY ISSUES

Accessibility issues present another notable limitation of conventional treatments. Factors such as geographical location, economic status, and healthcare infrastructure can significantly impact an individual's ability to access and afford traditional medical interventions.

In some regions, especially in developing countries, access to advanced medical treatments may be limited, leaving patients with fewer options for managing their health conditions. This disparity in accessibility can contribute to health inequalities and hinder the overall effectiveness of conventional treatments on a global scale.

LONG-TERM CONSIDERATIONS

Long-term considerations also play a crucial role in assessing the limitations of conventional treatments. While these interventions may provide immediate relief or control over certain conditions, their efficacy and safety over extended periods often raise concerns. For instance, prolonged use of certain medications may lead to drug resistance or tolerance, diminishing their effectiveness over time. Additionally, some treatments may address symptoms rather than the root cause of a medical issue, potentially leading to recurrent or chronic health issues.

Furthermore, the long-term impact of conventional treatments on the overall well-being of individuals is an area of ongoing research and consideration. For instance, the use of certain medications may be associated with an increased risk of developing secondary health issues or complications, necessitating a careful evaluation of the risks and benefits associated with extended treatment durations.

Conventional treatments, while valuable in addressing various health conditions, come with inherent limitations. Side effects can pose challenges to patients' comfort and well-being, accessibility issues may restrict certain populations from benefiting fully, and long-term considerations demand a careful evaluation of the ongoing impact on individuals' health. Recognizing these limitations is crucial for fostering a more comprehensive and patient-centric approach to healthcare that considers alternative and complementary strategies to address the diverse needs of individuals worldwide.

CHAPTER SIX

THE ROLE OF NATURAL REMEDIES
A HOLISTIC APPROACH TO HEALING

The holistic approach to healing is rooted in the belief that health is a complex interplay of physical, mental, emotional, and spiritual factors. Rather than focusing solely on treating specific symptoms or diseases, the holistic approach considers the individual as a whole. This perspective recognizes the interconnectedness of various aspects of a person's life and aims to address the underlying causes of illness rather than merely alleviating symptoms. Natural remedies play a crucial role in this holistic paradigm, as they often embrace a more comprehensive view of health and well-being.

COMPLEMENTARY THERAPIES

Complementary therapies are an integral component of the holistic approach, working in conjunction with conventional medical treatments to enhance the overall healing process. These therapies encompass a wide range of practices, such as acupuncture, herbal medicine, massage therapy, and yoga. The key principle is to complement mainstream medical interventions, promoting a synergy that considers both the physical and psychological aspects of health. By combining conventional and complementary approaches, individuals may experience a more comprehensive and personalized treatment plan that addresses their unique needs.

INTEGRATIVE MEDICINE

Integrative medicine represents a synthesis of conventional and complementary therapies, emphasizing the importance of collaboration between healthcare professionals from different disciplines. This approach recognizes that each individual may respond differently to various treatments and strives to create a cohesive, patient-centered strategy. Integrative medicine leverages the strengths of both conventional and alternative modalities, encouraging open communication between patients and their healthcare providers. This collaborative effort seeks to optimize health outcomes by considering the best available evidence from all relevant sources.

Natural remedies, as a subset of complementary and integrative approaches, play a vital role in promoting holistic health. Herbal remedies, dietary supplements, and lifestyle interventions are often central to these practices. The use of natural remedies is rooted in traditional knowledge and often involves harnessing the healing properties of plants, minerals, and other natural substances. Supporters argue that these remedies not only address symptoms but also aim to restore balance within the body, aligning with the holistic philosophy of treating the root causes of illness.

The holistic approach to healing embraces the interconnected nature of human health, considering physical, mental, emotional, and spiritual aspects. Complementary therapies work in tandem with conventional treatments, providing a more comprehensive and personalized approach to healing. Integrative medicine takes this collaboration further, promoting communication and coordination among healthcare professionals from various disciplines. Natural remedies, within this framework, offer a diverse range of options rooted in traditional knowledge and a holistic understanding of health and well-being. Ultimately, the integration of natural remedies into healthcare reflects a broader shift towards a more patient-centered, holistic approach to healing.

CHAPTER SEVEN

NATURAL REMEDIES FOR PTSD

IMPACT OF DIET ON MENTAL HEALTH

The impact of diet on mental health, particularly in the context of PTSD (Post-Traumatic Stress Disorder), is a multifaceted and significant aspect of holistic well-being. Research has increasingly highlighted the intricate connection between the foods we consume and our mental and emotional states. Individuals grappling with PTSD often experience heightened levels of stress, anxiety, and mood disturbances. Therefore, adopting a nutritious and balanced diet can play a crucial role in managing and mitigating the symptoms associated with this condition.

NUTRIENTS FOR MOOD STABILIZATION

Nutrition is a powerful modulator of mood, and certain nutrients are particularly noteworthy for their role in stabilizing emotions. For individuals with PTSD, achieving mood stabilization is a paramount concern. Omega-3 fatty acids, found in abundance in fatty fish such as salmon and flaxseeds, have been linked to improved mood and reduced symptoms of depression and anxiety. These essential fatty acids are integral to brain health and play a vital role in neurotransmitter function, potentially aiding in the regulation of mood disturbances associated with PTSD.

Similarly, incorporating foods rich in complex carbohydrates can contribute to mood stabilization. Whole grains, legumes, and vegetables release glucose gradually, providing a steady supply of energy to the brain. This can help prevent the energy crashes and irritability often experienced by individuals with PTSD. Furthermore, complex carbohydrates stimulate the production of serotonin, a neurotransmitter associated with feelings of well-being and happiness.

ANTI-INFLAMMATORY FOODS

The role of anti-inflammatory foods in managing PTSD symptoms is another crucial aspect of dietary considerations. Chronic inflammation has been implicated in various mental health disorders, including PTSD. Consuming a diet rich in anti-inflammatory foods can help counteract this process. Fruits and vegetables, especially those high in antioxidants, have anti-inflammatory properties. Leafy greens, cruciferous veggies, and berries are great options. Additionally, incorporating spices like turmeric, known for its potent anti-inflammatory effects, can be beneficial.

It's essential to note that personalized nutrition plays a pivotal role in addressing the specific needs of individuals with PTSD. While certain general principles hold, the optimal diet may vary from person to person. Consulting with a healthcare professional or a registered dietitian can help tailor dietary recommendations to individual circumstances, taking into account factors such as allergies, sensitivities, and pre-existing health conditions.

The impact of diet on mental health, the role of specific nutrients in mood stabilization, and the importance of anti-inflammatory foods are integral components of a comprehensive approach to managing PTSD. Adopting a mindful and nourishing diet can complement other therapeutic interventions, contributing to improved emotional well-being and overall quality of life for individuals dealing with the challenges of PTSD.

CHAPTER EIGHT

HERBAL REMEDIES

ADAPTOGENIC HERBS

Adaptogenic herbs play a significant role in traditional herbal medicine, offering a holistic approach to supporting the body's ability to handle stress and maintain balance. These herbs are known for their unique ability to adapt to the specific needs of the body, helping it cope with various stressors, be they physical, emotional, or environmental. Examples of adaptogenic herbs include ashwagandha, rhodiola, holy basil, and ginseng. These herbs are believed to regulate the adrenal glands and promote homeostasis within the body. By modulating the body's stress response, adaptogens contribute to overall well-being and resilience.

NERVINE HERBS

Nervine herbs, on the other hand, are valued for their calming and soothing effects on the nervous system.

They are often used to alleviate conditions related to stress, anxiety, and tension. Chamomile, passionflower, and valerian are well-known nervine herbs that have been used for centuries in traditional medicine to promote relaxation and reduce nervous irritability. Nervine herbs can be especially beneficial in supporting mental health, aiding sleep, and fostering a sense of tranquility. These herbs work by interacting with neurotransmitters and promoting a balanced nervous system function.

HERBAL TEAS FOR RELAXATION

Herbal teas for relaxation have gained popularity as natural remedies for managing stress and promoting a calm state of mind. Chamomile tea is a classic choice known for its mild sedative properties, helping to ease tension and induce a sense of relaxation. Lavender tea is another soothing option, with its aromatic compounds contributing to a calming effect on both the mind and body. Lemon balm and passionflower teas are also recognized for their relaxing properties, making them suitable choices for winding down after a hectic day. The ritual of preparing and sipping herbal teas itself can be therapeutic, adding to the overall relaxation experience.

Incorporating adaptogenic and nervine herbs into herbal teas for relaxation creates a synergistic blend that addresses both the physical and emotional aspects of stress. For instance, a blend of chamomile and ashwagandha can provide a soothing effect on the nervous system while also offering adaptogenic support for the body's stress response. Similarly, combining passionflower with rhodiola in an herbal tea can create a harmonious blend that promotes relaxation and resilience against stressors. Experimenting with different herbal combinations allows individuals to tailor their herbal tea experience to their unique needs and preferences.

The concepts of adaptogenic herbs, nervine herbs, and herbal teas for relaxation collectively showcase the diverse therapeutic potential of herbal remedies in promoting overall well-being. From adaptogens that enhance the body's stress resilience to nervine herbs that calm the nervous system and herbal teas that create a soothing ritual, these natural approaches offer holistic solutions for managing stress and fostering a balanced, relaxed state of mind.

CHAPTER NINE

MIND-BODY TECHNIQUES
YOGA FOR PTSD

Yoga has emerged as a powerful mind-body technique with significant benefits for individuals dealing with post-traumatic stress disorder (PTSD). The practice of yoga comprises a holistic approach, including physical postures, breath control, and meditation. For those suffering from the crippling effects of trauma, yoga acts as a therapeutic technique that treats both the physical and psychological components of their illness.

In the setting of PTSD, yoga offers a unique blend of asanas (physical postures) and pranayama (breathing techniques) to help patients reconnect with their bodies and minds. The physical postures of yoga give a disciplined mechanism for individuals to release tension and stored emotions in the body, generating a sense of grounding and stability. Additionally, the emphasis on controlled breathing in yoga helps regulate the neurological system, increasing relaxation and lowering the heightened state of alertness associated with PTSD.

The mindfulness aspect of yoga is particularly useful for those with PTSD. By encouraging practitioners to stay present at the moment and cultivate awareness of their thoughts and sensations without judgment, yoga provides a safe space for individuals to examine and process their traumatic experiences. This cognitive awareness, paired with the physical techniques, contributes to a gradual yet profound healing process.

MEDITATION & MINDFULNESS

Essential elements of mind-body practices that have become well-known for their therapeutic benefits on mental health include mindfulness and meditation. Originating in age-old contemplative traditions such as Buddhism, mindfulness entails purposefully focusing attention on the current moment while maintaining a non-judgmental mindset. People develop a greater sense of self-awareness by learning to notice their thoughts, feelings, and physical sensations through a variety of meditation approaches.

Mindfulness meditation is a useful tool for people who are dealing with stress, anxiety, or other mental health issues. By assisting people in breaking the pattern of dwelling and anxiety, the exercise fosters a more tranquil and balanced state of mind. Furthermore, mindfulness meditation has demonstrated its adaptability in clinical settings by being integrated into psychotherapy procedures like Mindfulness-Based Stress Reduction (MBSR) and Mindfulness-Based Cognitive Therapy (MBCT).

Mindfulness activities not only reduce stress but also enhance focus, emotional control, and general well-being. People can improve their relationship with their mental processes reduce reactivity and increase resilience in the face of life's obstacles by practicing mindful awareness of their thoughts and emotions.

BREATHING TECHNIQUES

A key component of many mind-body practices, breathing exercises are essential for encouraging relaxation, stress reduction, and general mental health. Because of their powerful effects on the autonomic nervous system, controlled and aware breathing techniques—known as pranayama in the yogic tradition—have been included in a variety of treatments.

Intentional patterns of intake and exhalation are used in deep breathing exercises to affect the body's stress response. Breathing deeply and slowly triggers the parasympathetic nervous system, which in turn promotes relaxation and lessens the physical symptoms of stress. This helps build long-term resilience against persistent stressors in addition to its instant relaxing benefits.

Breathing exercises also promote awareness and connection by acting as a link between the mind and body.

CHAPTER TEN

EXERCISE AND POST-TRAUMATIC STRESS DISORDER

ADVANTAGES OF PHYSICAL ACTIVITY

Exercise has been identified as a beneficial and all-encompassing strategy for addressing and reducing the symptoms of post-traumatic stress disorder (PTSD). Frequent exercise has advantages for more than just physical health; it's also important for resilience and mental health. A main benefit is the favorable influence on mood and emotional control. Getting moving promotes the release of endorphins, also known as "feel-good" hormones, which can help lessen the anxiety and depression symptoms that are frequently linked to post-traumatic stress disorder (PTSD).

Exercise not only has psychological advantages but also gives PTSD sufferers a sense of empowerment. Regular physical activity can assist to counterbalance emotions of helplessness and increase one's sense of control and accomplishment, which can lead to a higher overall sense of self-efficacy. This exercise's empowerment component fits in with the larger idea of trauma-informed care, which emphasizes the value of giving people the tools they need to actively participate in their healing.

EXERCISE TYPES

People with PTSD can benefit from a variety of exercises, and the choice of exercise may depend on the person's comfort level, physical preferences, and physical health. Aerobic exercises, like swimming, cycling, or jogging, have been demonstrated to improve mood and help lessen PTSD symptoms. These repetitive, rhythmic actions might have a relaxing impact on the nervous system, assisting in stress relief and relaxation.

Exercises for strength that involve resistance or weight-bearing can also be very helpful in treating symptoms of post-traumatic stress disorder (PTSD). Gaining physical strength can help with self-esteem and is generally associated with a feeling of increased resilience. The mind-body connection is emphasized through the unique combination of physical exertion and mental calm provided by yoga and mindfulness-based exercises. For those with PTSD, these techniques can be very helpful in lowering hyperarousal and fostering a sense of grounding.

FORMULATING A LONG-TERM FITNESS PROGRAM

For those with PTSD, developing a sustainable fitness regimen is essential because long-term effects depend on regularity. Establish attainable goals at first, taking into account the frequency and intensity of the activity.

To increase the possibility of adherence, it's critical to select activities that fit with personal tastes. Making exercise a regular part of one's routine can be achieved by adding physical activity into everyday activities like using the stairs, going for brisk walks, or playing leisure sports.

For people with PTSD, maintaining an exercise regimen is crucial. Support networks play a major part in this. The required accountability and motivation can be obtained by asking friends, family, or mental health specialists for their support and understanding. For people with PTSD, group exercise programs or other activities can provide a supportive environment by establishing a sense of community and shared experience.

Another important factor to take into account while creating a lasting workout program is adaptability. Realizing that circumstances, physical capabilities, and tastes might vary over time, people should be flexible in how they modify their fitness regimen. This adaptability makes it possible to continue incorporating physical activity into one's life, guaranteeing that it will always be a practical and helpful part of the overall plan for managing post-traumatic stress disorder.

CHAPTER ELEVEN

HYGIENE OF SLEEP

THE VALUE OF SLEEP

A vital component of human health, sleep is essential for many physiological and psychological processes. It is impossible to exaggerate how crucial getting enough good sleep is for maintaining general health, mental clarity, emotional stability, and even lifespan. The body performs vital functions like memory consolidation, immune system fortification, and tissue repair while you sleep. Numerous health problems, including an elevated risk of chronic ailments like obesity, diabetes, cardiovascular diseases, and mental health disorders, have been related to inadequate or poor-quality sleep.

Apart from its physiological advantages, sleep is essential for both emotional stability and cognitive function. A rested mind is more capable of focusing, picking up new information, and making decisions. On the other hand, a lack of sleep can negatively impact cognitive abilities, making it harder to solve problems, retain information, and control emotions. Sleep has a significant effect on mood; insufficient sleep is frequently linked to irritation, mood fluctuations, and an overall low emotional state.

CREATING A SLEEP SCHEDULE

A crucial element of excellent sleep hygiene is developing and following a regular sleep schedule. Establishing a regular sleep schedule is aiming to go to bed and wake up at the same time every day, including on the weekends. This aids in controlling the circadian rhythm, the body's internal clock that is essential to sleep-wake cycles. Maintaining a regular sleep schedule helps the body's circadian rhythm, which facilitates falling asleep and waking up feeling rejuvenated.

In addition to keeping a regular sleep pattern, you may tell your body when it's time to unwind by developing a calming habit before bed. This could involve doing things like reading a book, having a warm bath, or meditating or deep breathing as ways to unwind.

Since the blue light from electronics can disrupt the body's natural production of the sleep hormone melatonin, it's also critical to minimize screen time and steer clear of stimulating activities right before bed.

ALL-NATURAL SLEEP AIDS

The cornerstone of excellent sleep hygiene is creating a regular sleep schedule, however, some people may find that using natural sleep aids improves the quality of their sleep is beneficial. These tools frequently entail making lifestyle adjustments and forming routines that encourage calmness and restful sleep. Keeping a cozy sleeping environment is one such natural sleep aid. This entails purchasing a cozy mattress and pillows and maintaining the bedroom cold, quiet, and dark.

Popular natural medicines with relaxing properties are herbal teas, such as chamomile or valerian root tea. To encourage relaxation before bed, include these drinks in your routine. Furthermore, engaging in mindfulness practices and relaxation exercises like progressive muscle relaxation or guided imagery can assist in lowering tension and anxiety levels, which facilitates the transition from an active day to a peaceful night's sleep.

It's crucial to remember that everyone reacts differently to natural sleep aids, and speaking with a healthcare provider is advised especially for individuals who struggle with sleep issues regularly. Although natural sleep aids have their advantages, professional assistance may be necessary to address underlying sleep disorders or persistent insomnia to guarantee thorough and efficient therapy.

CHAPTER TWELVE

STRESS REDUCTION

RECOGNIZING SOURCES OF STRESS

One of the most important steps in effective stress management is identifying stressors. Stressors can take many different forms, such as demands at work, difficulties in personal relationships, financial difficulties, and health issues. If someone wants to address and lessen the negative effects of stress on their well-being, they must be aware of these triggers. People with this level of self-awareness can identify certain stressors and create focused coping and resilience techniques.

COPING TECHNIQUES

Effective stress management heavily relies on coping strategies. These coping strategies fall into several categories, such as emotion- and problem-focused coping. While emotion-focused coping seeks to control the emotional reaction to stimuli, problem-focused coping focuses on addressing the underlying source of stress. Developing good coping mechanisms like exercise, mindfulness, and reaching out to others might help people deal with challenges more skillfully. It's crucial to remember that everyone has a different set of coping skills, and developing a pattern for long-term stress management requires figuring out what works best for each individual.

DEVELOPING RESILIENCE

Enhancing one's capacity to overcome hardship is the goal of building resilience, a proactive approach to stress management. Creating a mindset that encourages adaptation and tenacity in the face of adversity is a key component of resilience. This can be accomplished by engaging in activities like encouraging optimistic thinking, keeping up a robust support system, and developing a feeling of purpose. Developing healthy habits and being committed to the process of building resilience will eventually increase a person's ability to tolerate stress and bounce back from it.

It becomes clear how coping strategies, resilience building, and stressor identification are related in the context of stress management. Recognizing stressors serves as the starting point for focused coping techniques, and over time, resilient coping tactics help build resilience. In a similar vein, developing resilience can improve a person's capacity to recognize stressors early on and utilize flexible coping mechanisms. This all-encompassing strategy highlights how crucial it is to handle stress on several levels to develop a thorough and long-lasting stress management strategy.